Jessica Rogers

My Life with Sacral Agenesis

A Children's Story

Illustrations by Melissa Rogers

www.isacra.org

This book is dedicated to all of the parents and children of iSACRA, the International Sacral Agenesis/Caudal Regression Association.

ISBN 979-8746804563

My Life with Sacral Agenesis

Hi! My name is Jessica, and I have curly red hair and freckles. I also have sacral agenesis, or SA for short. I'd like to tell you all about my life with sacral agenesis. You can meet some of my friends who have this same condition, too.

SA means the lower part of my spine didn't form. That happened before I was born. It's not anybody's fault; it's just the way I was born. Everybody is different. Nobody is really the same as anybody else.

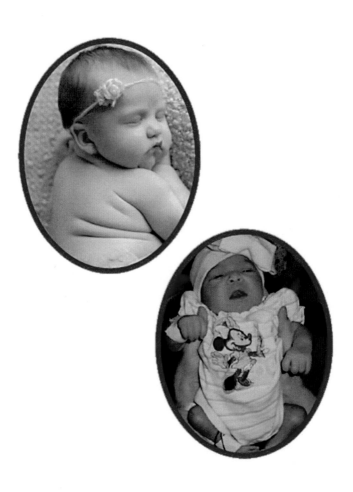

The bumps you can feel going down your back are the bones of your spine. Those bones are shaped like little rings and your spinal cord is inside those rings.

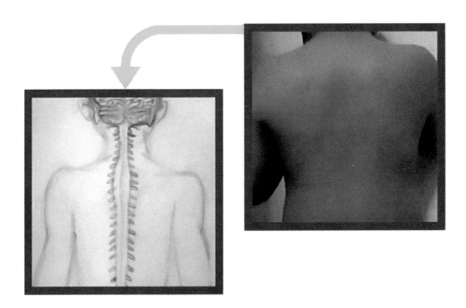

Your spinal cord connects your brain to the nerves all over your body. The spinal cord carries signals back and forth between your brain and different parts of your body so you can move and feel.

When part of the spine and spinal cord are missing, some parts of the body don't get signals to move or feel.

Some people with SA have a little part of their spine missing. You can see what is missing with an x-ray or other medical tests.

X-rays and other tests show if there is a little part missing, like this:

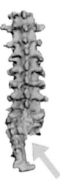

Missing part of the sacrum.

Or, a big part of the spine is missing like this:

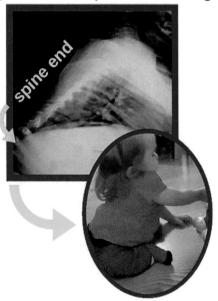

We are all a little different, even though we have the same condition.

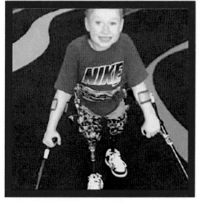

If people with SA have a lot of their spine missing, they usually can't move their legs very well. Sometimes their legs are very small and bent.

Others with SA may have legs that are small or stiff. Some can move their legs. It depends on what part of the spinal cord is missing.

If people with SA have only a small part of their spine missing, that might not show much on the outside. Sometimes the difference is only on the inside.

Sometimes parts of the body on the inside don't get brain signals to move. Medicines, surgeries, and some medical equipment can help those parts of the body work better.

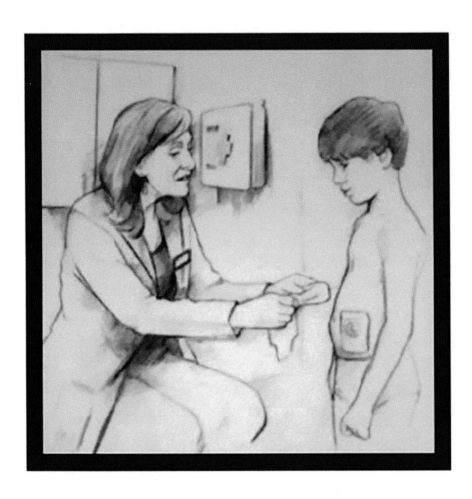

Some of us use wheelchairs, or we use braces, walkers, or crutches to walk, and some of us don't.

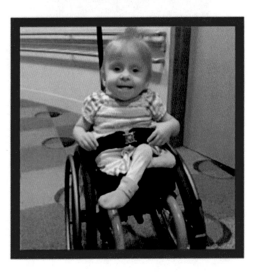

The important thing to know about all of us is that no matter how we move around, we can always get where we want to go!

We can do things you might not expect, like climbing the jungle gym, landing jumps at the skate park, playing basketball, and rock climbing!

Sometimes having SA is hard because you can't always do things just like other kids.

Also, some people might stare at you if you look different.

Taking medicine, getting sick, or having surgery is never any fun.

It's okay to feel sad sometimes. Everyone does when they are having a hard time.

But I can't stay sad for long. There are too many exciting things to do!

And it always feels great to achieve something that was really hard.

Sometimes doing things that are hard to do can make you better, or smarter, or stronger, or nicer. Can you think of an example where having SA might seem bad but then turn out to be a good thing?

When I was little, sometimes I wanted to be more like everyone else. But, I figured out how to do everything other people did. I just did those things a little differently.

I can run using just my hands and arms. I can race really fast in my wheelchair. I can even put roller skates on my hands and skate really fast.

Can you do this?

SA is a very rare condition. That means most people have never met anyone with SA before. If you have SA, it is easy to think that you are the only one.

But even if you have a very rare condition, you can still find a few other people who are a lot like you. Meeting new friends is a fun thing to do.

A lot of great things have happened to me that would not have happened if I was just like everyone else.

I got involved with sports. I became a good swimmer and a good wheelchair racer. Now, I travel all around the world to different races. It is so much fun!

Now, I am glad I am different. I am glad I am just me. I don't want to be anybody else!

Who knows what great things are going to happen for you in the future, just because you are you?

Here are some things I like to do. Check my list to see if you like any of the same things.

Swim
Play hide and seek
Play computer games
Go to birthday parties
Read stories
Go to the park
Play basketball
Eat ice cream
Race
Play with puppies
Watch TV
Watch movies
Jump on the trampoline
Go to the lake or beach
Ride bikes
Play with friends

Having SA doesn't stop us from making the most out of life. Come join us!

Make cupcakes

Paddle a boat

Play dress up

Enjoy a sunny day

Go shopping

Build sand castles

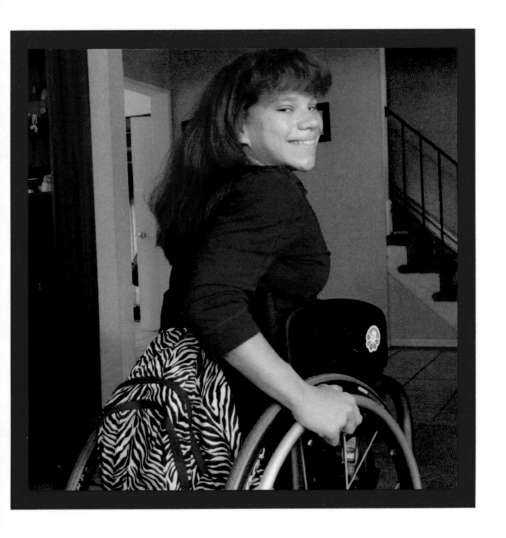

I hope you enjoyed learning about my life with sacral agenesis.

Your friend,
Jessica

www.isacra.org

For more information about sacral agenesis, visit
www.isacra.org.
For parents of children, or individuals with sacral agenesis or caudal regression syndrome, email us at
contact@isacra.org
to inquire about joining our active facebook group.

*i*SACRA provides support and information to persons with sacral agenesis/caudal regression syndrome and their families worldwide.

*i*SACRA promotes awareness and collaborates in research and advocacy to enhance the quality of life of persons with this condition and to advance medical knowledge.

*i*SACRA is here to help! Visit us at www.isacra.org for more information and opportunities to become involved.

Made in the USA
Monee, IL
23 May 2021